4/02

BRITISH RAILWAYS
STEAM
IN THE 1960s

BRITISH RAILWAYS
STEAM
IN THE 1960s

ERIC SAWFORD

ALAN SUTTON

First published in the United Kingdom in 1993 by
Alan Sutton Publishing Ltd · Phoenix Mill · Stroud · Gloucestershire

First published in the United States of America in 1993 by
Alan Sutton Publishing Inc. · 83 Washington Street · Dover NH 03820

British Library Cataloguing in Publication Data

Sawford, E.H. (Eric H.)
British railways steam in the 1960s.
1. Title
625.2610941

ISBN 0–7509–0139–X

Library of Congress Cataloging in Publication Data applied for

Endpapers: front: 'Castle' class No. 5094 Tretower Castle *arrives at Paddington;
back: Ivatt 2MT, No. 46410, outside the shed at Workington depot.*

Typeset in 10/12 Palatino.
Typesetting and origination by
Alan Sutton Publishing Limited.
Printed and bound in Great Britain by
WBC, Bridgend, Mid Glam.

Contents

A4 class No. 60008, *Dwight D. Eisenhower,* heading the 'Yorkshire Pullman' and awaiting departure at King's Cross.

9.61

Introduction

The year 1993 is an important milestone in railway history as it is twenty-five years since standard-gauge steam locomotives were operated in normal revenue service on British Railways. In those seemingly distant days it appeared that their replacements, such as the 'Deltics' class 40s, etc., would be with us for a great many years to come. Many of these classes have now been withdrawn for a considerable time, having given way to more modern forms of motive power.

In 1968, when British Railways steam was finally withdrawn, many enthusiasts lost all interest or turned their attention to industrial systems and other countries where steam was still in service. There was little to look forward to at this time, with only the legendary *Flying Scotsman* being permitted to operate on British Railways, and many dark clouds were on the horizon even for this famous locomotive. There was no prospect of any of the preserved locomotives being allowed to run on British Railways after steam finished. This remained the case for a considerable period of time.

Today we are fortunate in that not only have a large number of locomotives been restored, but some of those suitable can be seen in action on main lines. Others, after many years of restoration, are now nearing completion and will shortly be seen in action again, the majority on preserved railways.

The sixties commenced with steam still operating many express passenger services, the locomotives mostly being in fine mechanical and external condition. Famous examples include the Gresley A4s, still working prestige trains such as 'The Elizabethan'. Haymarket depot engines were a regular sight at King's Cross, and 'Top Shed' (King's Cross) locomotives were likewise commonplace in Edinburgh.

All this was soon to change as diesels rapidly took over the passenger work. Main-line locomotives were relegated to secondary routes, or specials and parcel traffic. Soon withdrawals became commonplace, and at an increasing rate the sad procession of withdrawn engines on their last journey was to become a regular sight. Many scrapyards sprang up throughout the British Isles, some dealing with their purchases almost as soon as received. Woodham Brothers at Barry, South Wales, built up a large number of locomotives. While it may have been a sad sight, it was responsible for many of the preserved examples that we see today. Without Barry the number of ex-British Railways locomotives existing would be much smaller.

This book is divided into five sections. In the first, many locomotives are seen in a condition much as they appeared in the fifties. In the background can often be seen examples of the diesels, then rapidly coming into service at an increasing rate.

Even during the first years of the sixties locomotives were to be found stored, withdrawn or out of use at depots, many not having worked for a number of years. This was by no means an uncommon sight. Some of those in this situation prior to 1965 are pictured in the second section. Generally only the 'Britannias' stored at March were to be returned to traffic for any length of time, in this case on the London Midland Region.

During the final four years of the decade, the remaining steam locomotives were rapidly being laid aside, stored or withdrawn. Those still in service were usually to be seen in an appalling condition, many with their name-, number- and smokebox-plates missing. Occasional shafts of sunlight to lift the depression were the 'specials' operated at this time. The locomotives concerned often received what was to be their last clean, and it was not unknown for this to be carried out by volunteer labour. Locomotives chosen to work 'specials' often came from a considerable distance. Some even travelled from the Scottish Region to the Southern, one in particular providing a superb performance. The locomotive in question was A4 class No. 60024 *Kingfisher*, at that time allocated to Aberdeen Ferryhill depot. The route chosen was from Waterloo to Weymouth. Anyone who travelled on the train in March 1966 will remember the run behind *Kingfisher* after it left Salisbury. Unfortunately this locomotive did not make it into preservation, ending its days in a North Blyth scrapyard the following year. Many other trains were also run at this time, with equally interesting motive power. It fell to the north of England to operate the final steam services, with many last runs and specials before the fateful day in August 1968 when the last British Railways steam locomotive worked in normal revenue service. Those active to the end on these workings were the class 5s, Standard designs and grand workhorses of the London Midland Region, the 8F 2–8–0s and, of course, 'Britannia' class No. 70013 *Oliver Cromwell*.

The fourth section shows some of the well-known restored and surviving locomotives of the nineties as they were to be seen during the sixties, many lying for years at Barry. For those photographed there in 1965 the prospects of any future work seemed beyond the realms of all possibility. One in this situation was *Duke of Gloucester*, photographed at Crewe prior to dispatch to Barry, and well illustrating this point. Now, after superb efforts by all concerned, this locomotive is one of the most popular of all the working examples. Having 'main-line approval' has enabled No. 71000 to work over the Settle and Carlisle line, and several other of the permitted routes.

In the final section are the sad and depressing sights of locomotive scrapyards. One in particular, Cohens of Kettering, which received a great variety of locomotives over the years, is featured. Many originated from the London Midland Region, but considerable numbers also came from the Western, Southern and Eastern Regions and were to end their days there.

Something that will become apparent to the reader is the short time that some locomotives remained in use. The last new steam construction was completed in 1960. The maximum time that any remained in service was just seven short years, such was the rush to replace them with diesels. In 1968 the first locomotive purchased from Barry was moved out, having spent only three years there. The last few to leave before closure remained for over twenty years, and they left in a very different condition to those fortunate enough to spend only a short time at Barry.

The sixties were certainly a decade of change, with a gloomy end for those interested in steam. Now, in retrospect, not all that happened then was to have a sad conclusion. This becomes apparent on seeing one of the superb preserved examples of British locomotive design in action, for instance when working hard on the 'Long Drag' of the Settle and Carlisle.

The Early Sixties

The 'Modernisation Scheme' introduced in 1959, together with the closure of many secondary and branch lines, had already had a considerable effect on the motive power situation at the beginning of the sixties. Further closures during the year and withdrawal of main-line passenger services from Marylebone to Sheffield on the old Great Central line were to add even more steam locomotives to those already surplus to requirements. Furthermore, diesel locomotives, multiple units and shunting locomotives were coming into service in ever-increasing numbers and, of course, the electrification of certain lines was taking place, especially in the south-eastern section of the Southern Region. All of these factors were greatly to reduce the number of duties carried out by steam locomotives.

Throughout the country, stored and withdrawn engines were already to be found at most depots. Prior to the sixties, those destined for scrapping were cut up at a locomotive works. The early sixties saw privately-owned scrapyards springing up in many parts of the country. These were to become an increasing feature of the decade, as not only locomotives but also coaches and wagons, etc. became surplus to requirements.

In spite of this, 1960 was the end of an era as the last new steam locomotives for British Railways was still under construction at the Swindon works. These were the powerful 9F Standard freight 2–10–0s. This class first made its appearance in 1954. It was one of the several Standard designs to be introduced during the fifties and was intended to have a considerable working life. This, of course, was to change in the headlong rush towards diesel locomotives.

Standard 9Fs were very much a part of the sixties scene. The design was mostly of a straightforward construction, although some very important variations were made in the case of ten members of the class: Nos 92020–29. These were constructed with Franco-Crosti boilers. The boilers were later replaced by others of a conventional type, but this batch of 9Fs remained easily recognizable. During 1959, various trials were made with Giesl ejectors, and one member of the class was fitted with this equipment. The first locomotives built experienced a certain amount of braking difficulties when working heavy goods traffic, especially if required to make unexpected stops. Trials were conducted on the east coast main line and the problems were soon rectified. In all, 251 9Fs were built over a seven-year period. The design incorporated 5 ft driving wheels and two outside cylinders with Waldschaerts valve gear. The boiler pressure was 250 lb per sq. in, and the combined weight of locomotive and tender was just over 139 tons. The last locomotives of this class were all Swindon-built, Nos 92218 and 92219 being completed in January 1960 and allocated to Bristol St Phillip's Marsh depot. The latter has survived into preservation and is to be found at the Midland Railway Centre.

The end of new steam construction for British Railways was in March 1960, when No. 92220 *Evening Star* was completed. This was the only member of the class to be named, the name being selected as part of a competition among Western Region staff. Unlike the other 9Fs, No. 92220 was turned out in passenger green livery with a copper-capped chimney. The naming ceremony for this important locomotive was held at Swindon on 18 March. From its first days in traffic, *Evening Star* was requested for special trains. Fortunately this very historic locomotive was earmarked for preservation as part of the National Collection, in recent years becoming very popular on specials. Some of the last 9Fs built were to remain in service for just six years before they joined the ranks of withdrawn locomotives awaiting their fate in scrapyards. The 9Fs, and of course the other

Standard designs, were capable of a great many years in service. The vast numbers of diesels, many built by private companies, were to seal the fate of steam. However, some of the diesel designs left much to be desired and were in a few years history themselves. Indeed, several were being withdrawn at the same time as the last steam locomotives.

One of the long-familiar wheel arrangements that was particularly hard hit at the start of the sixties was the 4–4–0. Locomotives of this type were frequently to be found on cross-country services and local stopping passenger trains. These duties were quickly taken over by diesel railcars, or lost completely due to line closures which were taking place at an ever-increasing rate. Locomotive withdrawals in the early sixties included many 2P 4–4–0s and Midland Compounds. The Southern Region also had a considerable number of 4–4–0s of various types in service during the fifties, while in Scotland many 'Glens', 'Scots' and 'Directors' had already been withdrawn. Inroads were also made into comparatively modern designs such as the 'Shires' and 'Hunts'. Many locomotives that still survived were to be found in store, unlikely ever to work again. All members of this class of 4–4–0s, officially known as D49s, were withdrawn in 1961.

Many tank locomotives previously used on suburban services, such as those that operated out of St Pancras, were replaced with diesels, thus making many Standard class 4MT 2–6–4Ts redundant. The trend was similar throughout the country. By mid-1960, nearly 850 engines were in store and withdrawals were increasing rapidly as the months went by. Locomotives such as the remaining 'King Arthurs' were included almost monthly in the withdrawal lists in the early sixties. Some of the old names were perpetuated. For example, many of the Standard 5s on the Southern Region received names previously carried by withdrawn 'King Arthurs', the entire class of which was out of commission by August 1962. Fortunately, one 'King Arthur' still survives – No. 30777 *Sir Lamiel*.

On the old Great Eastern territory the remaining 'Sandringhams' were rapidly being withdrawn, including the B2 Thompson two-cylinder rebuilds which were introduced in 1945. The 'Sandringhams' became extinct in August 1960.

For a great many years the 'Claud Hamiltons' were to be found throughout East Anglia, often, during the 1950s, working through to other regions on trains such as the Cambridge–Bletchley–Oxford services. The 'Clauds' were responsible for many of the local services in their last years. Only four remained in service at the start of 1960, and within eight months all had gone. The last survivor, No. 62613, was allocated to March depot for six months before withdrawal, and was condemned in August. Sadly, none has survived. The 'Clauds' and the 'Sandringhams' (assisted by the B12s) were responsible for most of the East Anglian services prior to the Second World War. One B12 4–6–0, No. 61572, outlived other members of the class by several months. It was purchased for preservation on the North Norfolk Railway where it is still in the process of a lengthy restoration programme.

On the brighter side, a number of veteran locomotives which had been preserved for many years were overhauled and put back into service in their pre-nationalization liveries. Among these were the Highland Railway 4–6–0 No. 103, and the Caledonian Railway 4–2–2 No. 123, magnificent in its blue livery. Another locomotive active at this time and, incidentally, the only one still to be seen on specials on the main line in the early 1990s, is *City of Truro*. Also active and restored were North British 'Glen' D34 class No. 256 *Glen Douglas*, Midland Railway 4–4–0 Compound No. 1000 and London and South Western T9 No. 120. The 'Glen' has recently been removed from the Glasgow Museum of Transport and transferred to a preservation site where it will be restored to working order. On completion this locomotive is bound to attract much attention.

Ever-increasing numbers of diesel locomotives appearing and taking over passenger traffic resulted in the withdrawal of some of the best-known Pacifics. Several Gresley A3s were withdrawn in 1961, only one, No. 60104 *Solario*, having been withdrawn previously. Those to go during this year included *Windsor Lad*, *Tagalie*, *Dayardo* and *Flamingo*. The latter was one of the rarest of all the A3s in the London area. Only after a Doncaster works visit was this locomotive likely to appear at King's Cross. *Flamingo* spent most of its working life at Carlisle Canal depot. Another of the early casualties was No. 60102 *Sir Frederick Banbury*, which was in fine external condition when it was withdrawn.

All the A4s managed to survive 1961. Even for those grand locomotives, however, the writing was on the wall, as the following year was to see inroads into this class. The first to be withdrawn in the October were No. 60030 *Golden Fleece* and No. 60033 *Seagull*. Before the end of the year, No. 60003 *Andrew K. McCosh*, No. 60014 *Silver Link* and No. 60028 *Walter K. Whigham* had joined them. All ended their days at Doncaster works, although none of them was actually cut up until the following year.

On the London Midland Region, withdrawals were to include six of the 'Princess' class Pacifics. The remaining members of the class struggled on until the end of 1962, when they too were withdrawn. Fortunately, two have survived: No. 46201 *Princess Elizabeth* and No. 46203 *Princess Margaret Rose*. This year was also to see the first of the 'Princess Coronation' class go, together with massive inroads into the 'Royal Scots' which had until then remained intact.

On the Western Region, 'Castles', 'Halls' and 'Kings' featured among the locomotives being withdrawn. The list of classes on all regions which had become extinct was growing rapidly. Among them were the Great Eastern 0–6–0Ts which had for many years been a familiar sight at Liverpool Street station and elsewhere. The last of the Fowler 0–8–0s, nicknamed 'Austin Sevens' by enginemen, and the Lancashire and Yorkshire 2–4–2Ts were all early casualties.

In Scotland, April 1960 saw the massive withdrawal of many long-serving classes. These included the unusual Great North of Scotland Railway 0–4–2Ts of classes Z4 and Z5, for so many years a familiar feature on the Aberdeen docks.

Closure of the motive power depots, inter-regional changes and shed-code renumbering were to become commonplace from 1961. Hornsey, like many large depots, closed during 1961, transferring some of its remaining allocation to King's Cross.

During 1962, further line closures were to take place. Certain locomotives that had been selected by British Railways were overhauled and repainted in pre-Grouping livery. Among them was a T9 4–4–0 built by the London and South Western Railway and repainted in that company's colours. Another locomotive so treated and delivered to the museum at Clapham was J69/1 0–6–0T No. 68633, finished in Great Eastern blue.

Early 1962 was to see the first withdrawals of another famous class, the Gresley V2 2–6–2s introduced in 1936. During the Second World War they performed many Herculean feats, often with only basic maintenance. Equally at home with passenger or goods traffic, the V2 certainly deserved its place in preservation. The one chosen, No. 60800 *Green Arrow*, was for many years a 'Top Shed' locomotive (King's Cross), appearing on expresses, fast freights and pick-up goods. During recent years this locomotive, restored to LNER green livery, has become a very popular engine on specials, with fine runs over the Settle and Carlisle and elsewhere.

One sight that was to become very familiar was the increasing dumps of withdrawn locomotives, not only at depots but also in sidings, etc. Eventually locomotives were sold for scrap and towed away on their last journey, only to be replaced by other withdrawn locomotives. The number of scrapyards dealing with these engines increased, and they were to be found in many parts of the country.

In spite of the approaching 'diesel era', modifications were still made to steam locomotives in the early sixties. The A3s had been fitted with double chimneys and many also received German-type smoke deflectors on works visits. Several members of the V2 class also received double chimneys which no doubt improved performance, but certainly did little for their appearance.

While railtours were common in the fifties, the next decade was to see an even greater number, most enthusiasts sensing that time was rapidly running out. One tour that attracted considerable attention in 1962 was a jointly organized venture by the Railway Correspondence and Travel Society and Stephenson Locomotive Society called 'The Aberdeen Flyer'. As the east coast main line was involved for the first section, nothing better than an A4 could be selected. That chosen was No. 60022 *Mallard*. The locomotive working right through to Edinburgh on a tight schedule, on time, arrival was unfortunately marred by a goods train wagon 'hot box' just before the border, delaying the trains following. From Edinburgh another famous A4 took the train to Aberdeen, this time one of Haymarket's 'Top Link' locomotives, No. 60004 *William Whitelaw*. Aberdeen was reached five minutes early. Then followed a railtour to Old Meldrum with restored Great North of Scotland D40 4–4–0 No. 49 *Gordon Highlander* and J36 No. 65345.

The return journey was over the west coast route with two 'Princess Royals': No. 46201 *Princess Elizabeth* to Carlisle and No. 46200 *The Princess Royal* for the final leg to Euston. As with many railtours, problems en route resulted in a very late arrival in London. Nevertheless, it was an adventurous tour, much enjoyed by the 250 participants.

The Final Years

By 1965 the railways presented a very different scene, whole areas having finished with steam and the rail network being considerably reduced. Many locomotive classes having become extinct, most of what was still in service were Standard designs and large well-known classes such as Stanier 'Black Fives', 8F 2–8–0s, etc.

The Scottish Region was still using steam on the Aberdeen to Glasgow service. Many A4s ended their working days on this duty, including some that had for years been King's Cross engines until the depot closed. One A4 so engaged was No. 60034 *Lord Farringdon*. Another among the last in service was No. 60024 *Kingfisher*. This was later chosen to work a special on the Southern Region, when it provided an exhilarating run. Just a few years later this A4 would have doubtless been a candidate for preservation, but this was not to be. It was withdrawn with No. 60019 *Bittern* in September 1966. *Bittern* does, of course, still survive.

The Carlisle Kingmoor depot was to become the last allocation of a considerable number of 'Britannias'. Their duties took them to Crewe, Leeds, Glasgow, etc., mostly on freight and parcels, with occasional passenger workings, replacing a failed diesel or operating a special working.

On the Southern Region, Bulleid Pacifics were still working most of the Bournemouth and West Country services, often in a deplorable condition with front number-plates and name-plates missing. Steam was also to be seen at Waterloo on stock workings. The last engine to receive repairs at Eastleigh works was 'Battle of Britain' class No. 34089, *602 Squadron,* amid considerable media attention. In July 1967 it was withdrawn, stored for a while and then in March 1968 it was despatched to South Wales where it was cut up along with many other Bulleid Pacifics. Steam working on the Southern Region had come to an end.

Enthusiasts had to travel to parts of the north-east and the north to see steam in regular use, by this time in a run-down and disgraceful condition in most cases. Locomotives that were chosen to work specials were cleaned. These were usually the only high points in a very dismal scene. Mechanical problems were often solved by cannibalizing withdrawn locomotives, and on shed visits it was often difficult to tell which locomotives were still in service, unless of course they were in steam. Everything was centred around diesels with their improved working conditions. To many enginemen, steam was old-fashioned and the quicker it vanished the better.

Some fine runs were still performed by steam during the last three years of the 1960s, especially on enthusiast specials. Among these were those covered by the few remaining 'Jubilees'. The one destined to be the last of the class in service, No. 45562 *Alberta*, was much in demand in its final years.

The remaining 'Britannias' in capital stock were withdrawn from Kingsmoor depot at the end of 1967, with one exception: No. 70013 *Oliver Cromwell*. 'Britannias' were the last Pacifics in service on British Railways. This last remaining example was kept busy in the final months on specials, parcels and goods traffic.

At the turn of what was to be the last year of regular steam operation on British Railways, activities were confined to the Liverpool, Manchester and Carnforth areas. Just fourteen depots were involved, if one includes the narrow gauge at Aberystwyth, which had steam locomotives on its books. Further closures in March, when three depots lost their allocation, and more on 4 May reduced the numbers even further.

January 1968 was to see 329 locomotives still remaining in service, with the most numerous being class 5s and Stanier 8Fs. Just three Ivatt 4MT 2–6–0 Moguls remained, the other locomotives being Standard designs, including the sole-surviving 'Britannia'.

Early in 1968, British Railways announced that it would consider steam specials only in areas where facilities still existed. These would only be permitted up to the last full weekend of steam working.

Sunday 4 August 1968 was destined to become an important day in railway history, when numerous specials were organized by various societies as well as British Railways. This caused considerable problems in routes, locomotive availability, etc., as, naturally, every organizer wanted to get as much variety as possible. There were, of course, only four classes available: Stanier 'Black Fives', Standard 5s, 8F 2–8–0s and *Oliver Cromwell*.

Many enthusiasts wanted one last run behind steam, as prospects of any change looked very unlikely at this time. My own choice was the 'Railway Correspondence and Travel Society End of Steam Rail Tour' which, although we had no idea when travelling on the west coast main line, was to be subjected to several problems and delays. This resulted in our return being almost four hours late! Many enthusiasts had difficulty getting home, or arrived back in the middle of the night.

Motive power on the 'RCTS' special for the first steam leg from Manchester Victoria was No. 73069 piloted by 8F No. 48476. Unfortunately the 8F was not in good condition, with a leaking tender causing an unscheduled water stop. At the time it was alleged that the Standard 5 was pushing the 8F as well as working the train.

On arrival at Blackburn the 8F came off and was replaced by Class 5 No. 45407, now one of the most famous 'Black Fives' in preservation, largely owing to its exploits on the West Highland line and superb runs when returning home. However, on 4 August No. 45407 was in a very different condition, with injector problems and not particularly clean. This was not the locomotive originally intended for this section, the locomotive originally booked being one that has survived into preservation, No. 45110, currently on the Severn Valley, but which had been commandeered for another train.

The final section of the tour was worked by No. 70013 *Oliver Cromwell*. As a result of many problems encountered on the trip, one section was curtailed. Had this measure not been taken, there is no knowing what time the train would finally have arrived back at Euston. It was certainly a memorable day, with considerable time spent standing still.

On 10 August, only five Standard gauge locomotives remained in service. These were three class 5s Nos 44781, 44871 and 45110, 8F No. 48448 and No. 70013 *Oliver Cromwell*. Three of these have been preserved: 44871, 45110 and 70013, which is on static display at Bressingham Steam Museum as part of the National Collection. This locomotive being kept in East Anglia is very appropriate as the 'Britannias' revitalized the area's services on their introduction.

British Railways operated the 'Last Steam-Hauled Special' on the fateful day of 11 August. Anyone who witnessed this even from the side of the line will recall the traffic problems – narrow roads and thousands of cars are incompatible. The resulting traffic jams in the Dales lasted for quite some time.

Shortly after working on the special *Oliver Cromwell* commenced its journey to East Anglia, travelling mostly at night. Transfer by road into Bressingham involved considerable planning.

At this time, steam enthusiasts were very much in the doldrums. However, British Railways still operated steam in the form of three narrow-gauge locomotives on the Vale of Rheidol. These were the only steam engines to receive the blue livery and large logo, which did nothing to improve their appearance.

Fortunately the situation was to change with preserved steam eventually being allowed to operate on certain lines. Much changed on the rail system of the British Isles during the ensuing twenty-five years, but that is a different story. To the enthusiasts of 1968, it was a black day when British Railways finished with steam. After all, steam power had been used since the beginning of railways. Many lost interest in railways. Steam was still in operation at various industrial locations, but, even here, many of the real veterans had been scrapped. On the Continent, steam could still be found at work, and considerable numbers of people made journeys to see what had previously been of little interest to most enthusiasts.

Although some of the preserved railways that we know and admire today existed in the mid-sixties, most were then only in the early stages of restoration. Over the years their numbers increased, the earlier ones going from strength to strength. Today, most people have steam locomotives operating not far from them at some time in the year. This fact provides a fitting tribute to British engineering.

The Scrapyard Era

For a great many years, most withdrawn engines were cut up at a locomotive works, often shortly after being condemned. Tenders were, on occasion, saved for use as water- and sludge-carriers or snowploughs. Many old examples of these were still in existence during the sixties, having survived the locomotive by a great many years. The scrap roads at most works were a Mecca to anyone on a visit, as locomotives which had seen little service in recent times were often to be found there, perhaps after languishing at the back of a shed for a considerable time.

While the works still disposed of some locomotives, the sixties was the era of the private scrapyard, many of which sprang up throughout the country. These were often sizeable companies, among them Cashmores, T.W. Ward, Motherwell Machinery and Scrap, Drapers and Cohens, most of which had sites at several locations.

Many of the scrapyard scenes in this book were taken at Cohens of Kettering over a long period in the sixties. They show examples of locomotives that ended their days at the 'Cransley Works' from the Southern, Western, London Midland and Eastern regions. Among these engines are many Standard designs, a considerable number having been in service for only a short time before being condemned. As with most of the scrapyards, many items of rolling stock, coaches and wagons were dealt with as well as locomotives. Kettering, for example, handled withdrawn London Transport equipment, locomotives from industrial concerns and many of the Oxfordshire Ironstone engines.

As withdrawals of steam locomotives increased, large dumps grew at many depots, often remaining for a considerable period. From time to time, batches of engines would be prepared for their final journey by dismantling valve gear and removing coupling rods. These were usually tied on to the running plate. After an oil round they started the slow journey to their last destinations, often some distance away. Such scenes became a familiar sight, although many were undertaken at night. Problems were frequently encountered en route – hardly surprising after months of lying around. Occasionally a locomotive was removed and dumped in a siding, or shunted into a motive power depot to receive attention before it could continue its journey. On arrival at the scrapyard, work was normally begun within a matter of days. This was less frequently so at Kettering, as there was usually a row of locomotives in the sidings with only two or three being dealt with at a time. Close study of the photographs suggests that there was no regular pattern in dealing with locomotives, although in all cases the firebox was left intact until the end. Unless one reads the caption first, some of the pictures require close study to decide what class the locomotive belonged too. Occasionally it was necessary to examine the valve gear and coupling rods (if they still remained) to determine the identity of a particular locomotive in a scrapyard. This method was not infallible, however, as parts were often exchanged, especially in later years. The engine number was usually to be found stamped onto each part.

By the time most withdrawn locomotives arrived at a scrapyard, items like front number-plates and cab-side number-plates (in the case of Western Region locomotives at least) had been removed. These, together with name-plates and smokebox number-plates, were offered for sale by the stores controllers of the region. Name-plates from light Bulleid Pacifics, 'Halls', etc. were available at what today seem ridiculously low figures, albeit reasonable sums at the time. Who would have thought that such items would fetch the price they do today!

On occasion, private scrap dealers such as Cohens would send staff to a locomotive depot to cut up locomotives that were considered unsafe to be towed away. Cohens dealt with a few engines at Eastleigh motive power depot.

By far the most famous of all the many scrapyards during the sixties was Woodham Brothers of Barry. This yard, just a few miles from Cardiff, was to attract many visitors over the years, unfortunately not all intent on looking and photographing. Without this yard the number of preserved locomotives still existing would be considerably reduced. Some of those rescued in later years represented an immense undertaking, in terms of both man hours and financial cost. In many cases, doubts were often raised as to whether a start would ever be made. Some, unfortunately, are still to be found very much in the condition in which they left Barry, or in a dismantled state.

Most of the engines dispatched to Barry were towed there by diesel locomotives. There were some exceptions that ran there under their own steam from nearby depots. The photographs of Barry were taken in October 1965. Most of the locomotives pictured are intact. Three years were to elapse before any were to leave the yard. Engine 4F 0–6–0 No. 43924 departed for the Keighley and Worth Valley, followed early in the next year by

Southern 'U' class 2–6–0 Mogul No. 31618. Those fortunate enough to make purchases early received a complete locomotive. This was not the case with those among the last to leave, which were robbed of parts and had deteriorated as a result of long exposure to the elements.

Unfortunately, not all arrivals at Barry were lucky, as over a hundred were broken up. Apart from Standard class 4 No. 76080 in 1972 and Great Western 2–8–0 No. 3817 in 1973, the cutting up of steam locomotives ceased during 1965 in order to deal with the vast number of wagons being received. Demolition was resumed in 1980 when a Western Region 2–6–2T Prairie and 9F No. 92085 were cut up. This, of course, gave an urgency to saving those remaining.

Probably the most remarkable preservation project, and certainly the most ambitious of all those involving engines rescued from Barry, was the Standard 8P Pacific No. 71000 *Duke of Gloucester*. The remains of this engine were dispatched from Crewe after the cylinders, valve gear, etc. had been removed. Photographs of this locomotive at Crewe awaiting removal give an idea of what was involved in the restoration. Fortunately this prototype, 1954-built engine is now in superb condition and one of the most popular of all those passed for main-line running.

Another example, which is still undergoing long-term restoration, is 'King' class 4–6–0 No. 6023 *King Edward II*. This locomotive, withdrawn in June 1962, was to remain at Barry until well into the eighties. This was largely because the rear pair of driving wheels had been cut, necessitating the very high cost of a completely new pair which have now been manufactured. This fine locomotive, now at Didcot, represents a long-term project, but one whose completion is eagerly awaited. Two other 'Kings' survive. The most famous of these is No. 6000 *King George V*, part of the National Collection. After a number of active years, this engine is now a static exhibit at Swindon Museum.

Various Bulleid Pacifics are nearing completion and will be seen in action once again during the next year or so. First on the scene will almost certainly be No. 34039 *Boscastle* at the Great Central Railway. Appearing soon after will be No. 34101 *Hartland*, No. 34081 *92 Squadron* and No. 34059 *Sir Archibald Sinclair*, all of which are well advanced. Others, however, are stored in the former British Railways works at Brighton or in the open air, waiting for work to start.

One of the quirks of fate is that only one ex-LNER type arrived at Barry. This B1 class locomotive, No. 61264, had been in use as a stationary boiler (numbered Departmental No. 29) and as a result was one of the last arrivals. It was rescued in 1976 and is still being restored. Had more ex-LNER types arrived in South Wales, doubtless they would quickly have been the subject of a preservation project.

The once very depressing sight of what was the largest British graveyard of steam locomotives has in recent years passed into history. This is a miracle in that so much of our railway history has as a result been saved from the cutter's torch.

Steam in Preservation

Quite a number of the preserved locomotives that operate today on main lines or at the many sites throughout the country were purchased direct from British Railways by individuals or groups, thus preventing them from ending up in a scrapyard. In the sixties only a handful of today's preserved railways were in operation, while others were in the early stages of organization and hardly in a position to purchase many examples. By this time many very interesting locomotive classes, some well worth preserving, had become extinct.

One of the well-known 'Merchant Navy' class, No. 35028 *Clan Line*, went direct into preservation. Others included the 1361 class 0-6-0ST No. 1366 and 'Modified Hall' class No. 6998 *Burton Agnes Hall*, which were to be seen at Totnes in 1967. Both of these are now at Didcot. There are, of course, many other notable examples, including *Flying Scotsman*, *Sir Nigel Gresley*, *Union of South Africa*, and the Adams Radial tank No. 30583, together with class 1400 0-4-2 tanks, etc.

In the case of the National Collection, those locomotives selected for preservation were earmarked well in advance of withdrawal. These, together with those already preserved over the years by the pre-nationalization railway companies, provided examples for the Railway Museum at Clapham. Several other important locomotives were purchased for static display at Butlins camps.

Many of the examples that are still with us today have been rescued from scrapyards, one yard in particular having made a particular contribution. This is owned by the famous Woodham Brothers at Barry, South Wales. As with most scrapyards, a huge amount of rolling stock was dealt with also. Not all locomotives that found themselves at Barry survived. Among these were several 5400 class 0-6-0 pannier tanks, a class designed for light passenger and push-pull work, and one class which has not survived into preservation. Doubtless the 5400 class would have been ideal for operation on many of the preserved railways.

The scrapping of locomotives at Barry was certainly well under way by the early sixties, with a considerable number of engines already broken up. After 1965, apart from odd examples of steam and diesel, attention was turned to the rolling stock. This arrived in huge numbers until 1980, when work was resumed on locomotives.

There were, of course, many setbacks: some locomotives were reserved, then cancelled, only to be taken over by another interested party; other engines were found to have major faults and others chosen in their place. Fortunately, all that remained have now left Barry. Only time will tell how many of the locomotives rescued will be fully restored.

Careful examination of the photographs taken at Barry in 1965 reveals that most of the locomotives at this time were in remarkable condition. In the case of the Great Western designs, the majority were complete, even to their copper-capped chimneys, safety-valve covers, etc. As time passed, this was no longer the case. Those remaining were reduced to rusty hulks, usually without chimneys, motion, cladding and even tenders in some cases, while all non-ferrous pipework, valves, etc. had gone long ago.

The purchase of some of the last locomotives must have been the easy part. Restoration to working order involved huge sums of money in both the overhaul of the remains and the replacement of the many missing parts. Many engines are still to be found very much in the condition in which they left Barry. If and when they will run again is in doubt. In some cases, engines were purchased as a source of spares with no intention of restoration, for example 'Castle' class No. 5043 *Earl of Mount Edgcumbe* and Jubilee No. 45699 *Galatea*.

Some of the locomotives that were still to be seen at Barry in the early eighties have now been fully restored. Notable among them is 'Battle of Britain' No. 34072 *257 Squadron* which was withdrawn from service in 1964. Another example is 'Merchant Navy' class No. 35027 *Port Line* which was officially withdrawn in September 1966. Both are now restored to a superb condition. One of the regions that has many survivors is the Western. This was helped greatly by the number of locomotives that were rescued from Barry. The 'Hall' class was a familiar sight in most parts of the region. Eleven members of this class have survived, although some are still in ex-Barry condition. The later 6959 'Modified Hall' class has seven examples, again with several in the process of restoration.

Heavy freight locomotives are always popular, especially when seen at the head of a loose-coupled freight – very reminiscent of times past. This interesting spectacle is now often provided at several of the preserved lines. The Western workhorse was the 2800 class 2–8–0, sixteen of which survive, including No. 2818, which is part of the National Collection. One is certainly left wondering if all of these engines will eventually be steamed again, since, in the years following their rescue, little or nothing has been done to several examples.

Surviving heavy-goods locomotives of the London Midland Region consist of a handful of Stanier 8F 2–8–0s and an ex–LNWR 0–8–0. The Eastern and North-Eastern Regions are represented by a few examples which are in the National Collection and the grand Q6 0–8–0 on the North Yorkshire Moors Railway. The Standard 9F 2–10–0 was a common sight on all three of these regions. Nine of these survive, including *Evening Star* which is at present at York Railway Museum.

In 1938, Collett introduced his 'Manor' class design for the Great Western Railway, principally for use on cross-country and secondary lines. In all, thirty locomotives were built, some prior to the Second World War and the remainder in 1950. Nearly a third of this very useful class has survived. Nine examples are distributed over several sites, the Severn Valley Railway being home for three. Several are completely restored, in some cases now awaiting repairs after several years of service. The remaining examples are all well under way, and hopefully all nine will be in working order in the near future.

The Bulleid Pacifics are among the most popular of all the preserved passenger locomotives. Some of those that have 'Main Line Approval' have put up some spectacular performances in recent years, especially the unrebuilt 'West Country' No. 34092 *City of Wells*, and the rebuilt No. 34027 *Taw Valley* and 'Merchant Navy' No. 35028 *Clan Line*. Fortunately, Barry received a considerable number of these locomotives. Two were broken up: 'West Country' class locos No. 34045 *Ottery St Mary* and No. 34094 *Mortehoe*. However, by far the largest number survived, albeit often spending a considerable number of years exposed to the salt-laden atmosphere. Three Light Pacifics are now in the final stages of restoration, and all are expected to be operational within the next two years. Several 'Merchant Navy' class locomotives have already been restored. Those that have not are either in the early stages of restoration or still waiting for work to start. None are likely to be completed within the next two or three years.

Work is being done on a great many other locomotives. In some cases progress is rapid, in others it is very slow, depending on funds and labour commitment. Certainly a great many still exist where either work has yet to begin, or only cosmetic work has been carried out for display purposes. Every so often another long-withdrawn example is completed and hits the headlines in the railway press. But the story does not end there. Steam locomotives must be maintained and subjected to periodic overhaul, all of which takes capital and calls for considerable commitment on the part of helpers. This is exemplified by the restoration of, without doubt, one of the most popular of all the preserved engines: A4 class No. 60007 *Sir Nigel Gresley*. This has now undergone another very costly major overhaul in preservation and has returned to action once again on the main line.

1 Steam's Swan Song, 1960–1964

8F No. 48612 was going in fine style as it tackled Shap, banked in the rear by a Fairburn 2–6–4T from Tebay shed, where the banker would have been requested. At this time the majority of goods traffic was still steam-hauled. Most of the passenger trains had been taken over by diesel locomotives.

9.63

A1 class No. 60136 *Alcazar* had already shut off steam as it passed Walton crossing on the approach to Peterborough. Note the Travelling Post Office line-side equipment. Just visible farther to the left is the Leicester line. *Alcazar* was based at Doncaster from 1958 until withdrawal five years later.

Pannier No. 4689 shunts empty coal wagons at Coleford junction. These sturdy shunting tanks were to be found throughout the Western Region on a variety of duties, including local passenger services. Several were to be purchased by the National Coal Board and London Transport. Some of these, on withdrawal, passed into preservation.

25.10.64

Early autumnal mist softens the background as No. 60006 *Sir Ralph Wedgwood* speeds through Huntingdon at the head of a northbound express. This King's Cross A4 was one of those to end its days working from Aberdeen depot. It was withdrawn from there in 1965.

Several of the 'Britannia' class locomotives formerly based at Stratford were transferred to Immingham depot when their duties were taken over in East Anglia. One duty which they had in turn taken over from Immingham's B1s was the King's Cross–Cleethorpes service. Here, No. 70040 *Clive of India* has just left Huntingdon. The Immingham 'Britannias' were transferred to Carlisle (Kingmoor) where they ended their working days.

4.10.62

This Stanier 8F 2–8–0, No. 48656, was one of the class allocated to Bletchley depot. For years the depot had a fair number of veteran LNWR 0–8–0s in its allocation. These were renowned for their wheezing and whistling sounds.

30.6.63

New England depot had a repair shop attached to the main building. The shop usually dealt with fairly minor repairs on two or three locomotives at a time. Standard 9F 2–10–0 No. 92171 is receiving attention to its motion. It was among the last locomotives to have repairs carried out in the New England workshop.

30.8.64

Standard 5 No. 73070 marshalls locomotives for their next duties, with a Great Western 'Manor' class next in line at Shrewsbury depot. Several of the latter were active at the depot in 1964. No. 73070 was allocated to Chester at this time. It was to move to Bolton from where it was withdrawn in May 1967. Construction of this class continued until June 1957, many completing just ten years in service.

7.64

Workington was home for a considerable number of 4F 0–6–0s, three of which are shown here. Nearest the camera is No. 44035, and No. 44305 is in the background. Workington usually had an allocation of six of these very useful locomotives. One wonders if two 4Fs with similar numbers occasionally caused problems when rostering engines.

9.63

At several locations on the Eastern Region it was usual for an express locomotive to be on stand-by duties, possibly to pilot an ailing engine or, if necessary, take over the train completely. V2 No. 60880 was on just such a duty at Peterborough. Note the double chimney. This no doubt improved performance, but did little for the general appearance of the V2s.

6.9.62

Pannier tanks were often to be found on passenger services. No. 9669 is seen here on such a duty at Bala. This class was the most common on the Western Region, with well over eight hundred in service scattered throughout the British Isles. Panniers are represented in preservation by sixteen examples.

27.6.62

Class 5 No. 45373 shunts dead engines at Skipton, including B1 4–6–0 No. 61016 *Inyala* and 4F 0–6–0 No. 44222. Movements such as this were often welcomed by photographers, since locomotives inside the depot and in impossible photographic positions usually appeared outside for only a few brief moments before returning to the inner depths of the shed.

A3 No. 60102 *Sir Frederick Banbury* speeds through Huntingdon with a northbound fast freight, including a loaded cattle wagon next to the engine. In spite of external appearances, No. 60102's days were numbered as it was withdrawn during the following month. This A3 was one of those not to receive German-type smoke deflectors.

14.9.61

'Castle' class No. 5045 *Earl of Dudley* runs into Paddington at the head of an express from Worcester. This class was first introduced by the Great Western in 1923, with a further batch built after the war. Fortunately, several examples survive into preservation. Those that have been restored are very popular engines on special trains.

'King' class No. 6008 *King James II* leaves Paddington on its way to Old Oak Common depot for servicing, having been released from its train by one of the Paddington 6100 class station pilots. This class consisted of thirty locomotives introduced to a Collett design for the Great Western Railway in 1927. A double chimney had been fitted to No. 6008.

A1 class Pacific No. 60157 *Great Eastern,* pictured here at York MPD, had less than a year remaining in service. This locomotive was one of the five members of the class fitted with roller bearings. No. 60156 was a Doncaster engine at this time, having been for several years, prior to 1959, at 'Top Shed', King's Cross.

2.5.64

Banbury shed was always an interesting location until the end of steam, as a variety of locomotives was usually to be seen. Here, 'Modified Hall' class No. 6979 *Helperly Hall* appears to be ready to work a passenger train, judging by the lamps above the buffer beam.

These massive 2–8–2Ts were designed for heavy freight use, being rebuilds of 4200 class 2–8–0Ts with extended bunkers and trailing wheels. No. 7207 was active at Banbury. It was still carrying both front and side number-plates when photographed, even though many locomotives had lost one or other at this time. However, no shed-plate was carried. Three examples of this class have been preserved.

9.63

11

2MT No. 46455, employed on the Penrith to Keswick goods, had no return working. It is seen here leaving Keswick with only a brake van. This once-busy route through to Workington was only open as far as Keswick at this time.

9.63

'Jubilee' class No. 45627 *Sierra Leone* speeds across Anglesey on its way to Crewe. Withdrawal of this class started in 1960, a considerable number went during 1962 and the last survivors hung on until 1967. The last to be withdrawn was No. 45562 *Alberta*. This was taken out of service in November 1967.

6100 class No. 6146 on station pilot duties at Paddington. This class was very familiar on local passenger trains and pilot duties in the London area for a great many years, with a large number being allocated to Old Oak Common depot. The 6100s first made their appearance in 1931, having been built for the duties mentioned above.

A1 class No. 60146 *Peregrine* takes water at its home depot at York. Steam locomotives were still very active in the north at this time, although diesels were in charge of most expresses. A class 40 D347 is in the background. These engines are now history themselves, although examples are preserved. Unfortunately this is not the case with the A1s.

2.5.64

2MT No. 46520 appeared to have worked a summer special into Pwllheli when pictured at the depot. The locomotive is still carrying the reporting number 2J39. Several examples of this class were used on this line from the late fifties onwards, taking over some of the duties previously worked by 'Dukedog' 4–4–0s.

27.6.62

01 class No. 63746, pictured at March. At the end of 1963 this depot closed to steam, the remaining locomotives, including No. 63746, mostly going to Staveley (41C). Note the coaling plant in the background, a familiar fen country landmark for miles around during steam days.

28.7.63

One of the most modern locomotive classes to work over the Mid-Wales line were these Standard 4MT 4–6–0s. No. 75020 is an example of the design fitted with a double chimney in green livery. Here it is pictured at Pwllheli, awaiting a return working to its home depot at Machynlleth.

27.6.62

A3 No. 60083 *Sir Hugo* was a Newcastle engine which was for a number of years based at either Heaton or Gateshead depots. During this time it was a frequent visitor to London, often appearing at the head of services taken over at short notice. Here the locomotive is heading north at the head of a semi-fast leaving Huntingdon.

3.3.63

The driver of class 5 No. 45323 had decided not to call on the service of a banker on Shap. The locomotive is blasting its way towards the summit. The wild, open spaces of Shap in winter can be very inhospitable, especially in high winds and driving snow.

9.63

Another of the Standard designs of which no example now exists was the 77000 series 3MT 2–6–0 Mogul. Undoubtedly these would have been ideal locomotives for a number of preserved lines. No. 77000 stands in Darlington shed yard. This was a small class based for almost its whole working life in the north-east and Scotland.

2.5.64

Working the 'London North Eastern Flyer' was undoubtedly the swan song for A3 No. 60106 *Flying Fox*, which put up a very creditable performance and lived up to its name. The A3 is here entering Peterborough where it took water. Note the Gresley coaches. No. 60106 was a New England locomotive at this time, King's Cross MPD having closed in 1963. Prior to 1963, No. 60106 had been a Grantham engine for several years.

2.5.64

Numerous enginemen are to be seen in this picture as No. 60106 takes water at Peterborough. This A3 was withdrawn from service just seven months later and dispatched to King's scrapyard at Norwich for cutting up, where several other New England A3s ended their days.

2.5.64

Clean locomotives were the exception during the mid-sixties. 'Modified Hall' class No. 6994 *Baggrave Hall* was in fine external condition and is seen here being shunted at Banbury. Note that it is fitted with a straight-sided tender. Judging by the locomotive's general appearance it would seem highly likely that it had recently received works attention.

This fine example of the Stanier class 5 remained in service for almost twenty-one years. Seen here at March depot, No. 44919 was a Saltley depot locomotive (21A). London Midland Region engines were often seen at March from various Midlands depots. This one was completed in December 1945 and withdrawn from service in December 1966.

Tebay depot's allocation was usually in the region of ten locomotives, most of which were bankers. Here, two of those employed on these duties are standing outside the shed: Fowler 2–6–4T No. 42414 and Fairburn 2–6–4T No. 42110. The Fowler locomotive is one of the batch with side-window cabs.

18.9.64

'Britannia' No. 70007 *Coeur-De-Lion* was among the most active members of the class while allocated to March, being employed on a wide range of duties. Most of the class at the depot were allocated there for just over two years before transfer to the London Midland Region. This one went to 12A Carlisle Kingmoor where it remained until its withdrawal in June 1965.

14.7.63

The 'Grange' class was introduced in 1936. Designed by Collett, these versatile mixed traffic 4–6–0s were very similar to the 'Halls', one major difference being their 5 ft 8 in driving wheels as opposed to the 6 ft wheels of the 'Halls'. Eighty locomotives were built, and some parts were incorporated from withdrawn 4300 class 2–6–0 Moguls. No. 6874 *Haughton Grange,* here at Banbury, was a Didcot locomotive at this time.

9.63

This 5100 class 2–6–2T Prairie, No. 4142, was lying out of use at Banbury and, judging by appearances, was unlikely to work again. This locomotive is one of the batch rebuilt from 3100 class 2–6–2T Moguls. Some later members of the class were built from scratch.

9.63

At Darlington depot an A3 Pacific was usually to be found in steam to cover any locomotive failures. Here, No. 60045 *Lemburg* was on this duty, in the A3's final form – with double chimney and German-type smoke deflectors. *Lemburg* was withdrawn in December 1964 and was cut up at Drapers Hull.

2.5.64

One of the workhorses of the north-east, pictured here at Darlington, was Q6 No. 63410. The Q6 was a powerful 0–8–0 heavy freight design introduced by Raven for the North Eastern in 1913, with 120 members of the class to be found throughout the north-east. Fortunately one, No. 63395, has been preserved on the North Yorkshire Moors Railway.

2.5.64

Immaculate 'Castle' class No. 5094 *Tretower Castle* arrives at Paddington with an express. Note the large reporting numbers carried by the Western Region trains. This Gloucester locomotive was certainly a credit to the depot.

The Drummond M7 class 0–4–4Ts introduced by the London and South Western Railway in 1897 were for a great many years a familiar sight at Clapham junction on carriage duties. A few were still active in the early sixties. Nine Elms had a number in its allocation, the Clapham junction duties being covered by this depot.

Standard class 5 No. 73112 arrives at Clapham junction with empty stock. The locomotive was allocated to 70A Nine Elms for a considerable number of years. It was later called *Morgan Le Fay*, the name once carried by a 'King Arthur' class 4–6–0, No. 30750.

9.61

Class 5 No. 45284 coasts down Shap with a train that would appear to be carrying coiled steel products of some type. While in summer this was doubtless a pleasant experience, it would have been very different in winter in a howling gale and driving rain or snow when crossing the wild and exposed Cumberland Fells.

9.63

The 'Jinty' was among the most widely known of all the LMS designs on the London Midland Region. Indeed, you could not travel far without encountering at least one or two. These sturdy 0–6–0Ts have been well represented in preservation by ten examples, although not all are in running condition. This member of the class, No. 47427, is pictured at Skipton.

On a cold Boxing Day morning, A3 No. 60075 *St Frusquin* heads a southbound parcels train near Abbots Ripton. The freezing conditions created an effective smoke screen. This A3 spent many years allocated to Gateshead depot, from where it was withdrawn in April 1964.

12.61

Standard 9F No. 92020, one of the batch built with Franco-Crosti boilers, at Kettering coaling plant. In their later years they were rebuilt to conventional design, as seen here. Several ended their working days in the Birkenhead area.

13.12.64

B1 No. 61159 simmers gently in the yard at March. Note the water crane, complete with coal-burning stove for prevention of freezing in severe weather, and the rails which were, as in many depots, heavily coated with a mixture of oil, grease and coal dust. The B1 class introduced by Thompson for the LNER in 1942 was a popular design with the enginemen, and capable of handling express trains on tight timings, as Immingham depot's B1s proved in the late fifties on the London turn.

21.7.63

The tender of veteran 'Caledonian Standard Goods' 2F 0–6–0 No. 57302 had been well and truly topped up as it performed shunting duties at Dumfries. Pre-Grouping designs were rapidly being withdrawn at this time, many having lain idle or been stored at depots for a considerable period.

9.63

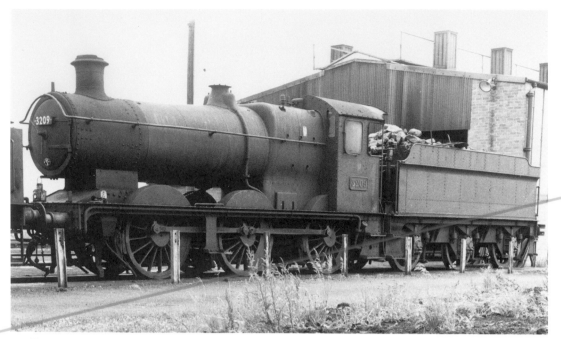

Pwllheli was a sub-shed of 89C Machynlleth. As a result it did not have a regular allocation of its own, four or five locomotives being outstationed and changed at regular intervals. Class 2251 No. 3209 was at the depot in the company of 2MT No. 46520.

27.6.62

'Jubilee' class locomotives were often to be found at Llandudno depot, many having worked in on special summer services. No. 45697 *Achilles* was a Leeds Holbeck engine. This was among the last 'Jubilees' to remain in service, being withdrawn from Holbeck in September 1967 and cut up at Cashmores Great Bridge in 1968.

12.7.64

Standard class 9F 2–10–0 No. 92040 of New England depot had been given the main line from Huntingdon. The 9F was in charge of a long train of coal empties which it was handling in fine style on the long drag up to Abbots Ripton.

14.3.63

O2 class 2–8–0s were once a very familiar sight at March depot, although by this time they were becoming rare. No. 63926 was built in 1921 by the North British Locomotive Company, then later rebuilt with a side-window cab. It ended up being classified as O2/4. The last year in which the remaining O2s were in service was 1963. Thirty were withdrawn in September (including No. 63926) and the last five in November.

23.6.63

Two roads within Bletchley depot were set aside for repair work, and many types of locomotives received attention over the years. Here, 8F No. 48493, a Bletchley locomotive undergoes repairs. The depot closed to steam on 5 July 1965.

Judging by the smoke screen trailing behind 'Royal Scot' No. 46101 *Royal Scots Grey*, this engine was not in the best condition as it crossed Anglesey en route to London from Holyhead. No. 46101 was a Camden engine at this time. It was later transferred to Willesden depot, then withdrawn in 1963.

'Merchant Navy' No. 35013 *Blue Funnel* roars through Clapham junction on its way to Waterloo. This was an Exmouth junction depot engine at the time. It was withdrawn in 1967 and ended its days in South Wales.

9.61

Shafts of weak, late autumn sunshine highlight parts of 8F No. 48204 standing in Wellingborough shed as it receives attention to its running gear. The Stanier 8Fs had a long association with Wellingborough, where among their duties were the heavy iron ore trains originating from the once extensive workings in the area. Indeed, most of Wellingborough's allocation in steam days consisted of heavy freight locomotives.

A4 No. 60033 *Seagull* leaves King's Cross at the head of the 'Tees-Tyne Pullman'. Within a short time these duties were passed on to diesels, with the recently introduced 'Deltics' handling many of the important express trains. *Seagull* was one of the first A4s to be withdrawn, and was taken out of service from King's Cross depot in October 1962.

9.61

'Manor' class No. 7809 *Childrey Manor* and Standard class 2MT No. 78003 await their next duties at Aberystwyth depot. The 'Manors' were designed for use on secondary lines by the Great Western Railway in 1938 to a Collett design. For many years they were employed on the principal passenger trains on the mid-Wales lines.

7.61

New England depot had a sizeable allocation of V2s, which could be seen on a wide variety of duties from express passenger, semi-fasts and parcels to heavy mineral trains. No. 60948 is seen here with a train of flat wagons.

28.3.63

The J94 class was a Ministry of Supply design introduced in 1943. It was designed by Riddles, who also introduced the WD 2–8–0 and 2–10-0. Seventy-five of these sturdy 0–6–0STs were purchased in 1946 by the LNER, mostly being used in the north-east to replace ageing locomotives. No. 68060 was a Darlington engine, pictured here in the works yard.

2.5.64

'Britannia' No. 70008 *Black Prince* was in trouble as it struggled through Beattock station with a northbound express. This 'Britannia' was originally a Norwich engine, later transferred to March and then on to the London Midland Region at Carlisle depot during 1963. The problem with No. 70008 was not serious and it remained in service for another three years.

18.9.64

O1 class 2–8–0s were among the last heavy goods engines allocated to March. The O1s were introduced in 1944 by Thompson, with 100A boilers and Walschaerts valve gear. At the start of the sixties, March had twenty-five members of this class in its locomotive allocation. This figure was gradually reduced by withdrawals and transfers, with only a few left by 1963.

Standard 3MT No. 82008 at Barmouth. At this time, 82000 series 2–6–2 tanks were employed on many of the passenger services. In their last years, members of this class was also to be seen on empty stock workings at Waterloo and elsewhere.

7.61

Rebuilt Patriot No. 45526 was only just still in service when at Carlisle Upperby. The following year it was withdrawn from service. Note the diescl on the adjacent line, diesels having taken over all the regular passenger trains. The few remaining express locomotives worked the odd special, parcels and even goods traffic.

18.9.64

The Peterborough to Leicester services were once the domain of the 2P 4–4–0s. These gave way to more modern motive power in the form of Standard class 4MTs. No. 75040 is pictured near Walton, Peterborough. This locomotive was one of several in Leicester depot's allocation.

This interesting study of Class 5 No. 44769 shows how many of these locomotives were to be seen in service during the sixties in a rather unkempt condition. This engine was built in April 1947, remaining in service until June 1965. It was typical of many members of the class, spending just eighteen years in service.

'Hall class' No. 5923 *Colston Hall* was one of the class allocated to Oxford depot and is seen here in the yard of its home depot. The 'Halls' and the later 'Modified Halls' were to be found in the allocation of a great many Western Region depots, with a number always to be found at Oxford in steam days.

Another of the surviving J27s to be seen at York was No. 65844, as with No. 65894 in fine external condition. Most of the locomotives present at York shed were of much later designs, including a number of Standard class designs and 8Fs. One of the latter, No. 48533, is in the background.

2.5.64

When the 'Britannias' were replaced by diesels at Norwich, most were transferred to March depot, together with some from Stratford shed. No. 70009 *Alfred the Great* was originally a Norwich locomotive. After approximately two years at March, this engine was allocated to Carlisle (Kingmoor) depot where it remained until withdrawn from service early in 1967.

A3 No. 60054 *Prince of Wales*, pictured at King's Cross. Note the run-down condition, the smokebox door clearly showing hard running. Although fitted with a double chimney, the German-type smoke deflectors had still to be fitted. This was done the following year. The locomotive remained in service until July 1964.

9.61

Work-stained, with front number- and depot-code-plates missing, Standard 5 No. 73158 presents a disgraceful sight at Bedford. This locomotive was eventually to become one of the batch allocated to Patricroft, from where it was withdrawn in October 1967.

30.6.63

A 4F 0–6–0 workhorse No. 44570, and 0–6–0T 'Jinty' No. 47454 at Skipton depot. Just visible inside the shed is a Standard 2MT tank. Skipton depot was not large, having in the region of thirty-five to forty steam locomotives before diesels made their presence felt.

9.63

'Crab' No. 42914 fills up before leaving the Scottish Region depot of Dumfries. These very useful 2–6–0 Moguls were introduced in 1926 by Hughes for the LMS. Of the 245 examples, some were among the last steam locomotives operating from Birkenhead depot. During their long years in service, 'Crabs' were to be seen on varied duties, including passenger trains on many occasions.

Giving a true impression of power, work-stained 9F 2–10–0 No. 92006 awaits its next duty at York. This locomotive was one of the batch fitted with a double chimney. Built in 1959, it was to remain in service for a comparatively short period – an unfortunate victim of the modernization plan.

The 'wheel tapper', inspection lamp and hammer in hand, stands ready as A4 No. 60034 *Lord Faringdon* runs into King's Cross at the head of the 'Tees-Tyne Pullman'. On the left can be seen the small inspection shed at the King's Cross engine point with a diesel locomotive inside. *Lord Faringdon* ended its working days at Aberdeen and was withdrawn in September 1966.

9.61

Having made what was almost certainly its last works visit, Standard class 4 No. 75006 stands in the yard of Darlington depot resplendent in lined green livery. This 4MT was among the first Standard designs to make their appearance in 1951. Of the eighty built, six examples of these popular engines are in preservation, but No. 75006 is not among them.

Workington depot, with a rather grimy Ivatt 2MT, No. 46410, outside the shed. This very useful class was introduced by the LMS in 1946. The first five were allocated to Kettering where they replaced veteran Midland 0–6–0s on the Kettering–Cambridge service and on other duties. As more were delivered, they were to become commonplace throughout the London Midland Region, later finding their way into other areas.

9.63

This interesting front-end study shows the mixed traffic locomotives of the London Midland and Eastern regions, at March depot. The class 5 on the left, No. 44981, is a 1946-built example of the 842 constructed. The B1 No. 61003 *Gazelle* is one of the first locomotives built of this 410-strong class, introduced by the LNER in 1942.

Here, most of the occupants of the roundhouse at Wellingborough depot are diesels. Standard class 2MT No. 84005 was still active and receiving attention. It was also in a very reasonable external condition. No original member of this class has survived, although several of the very similar 2–6–0 Mogul tender design are preserved.

8.11.64

Occasionally, B1 class locomotives were to be seen fitted with self-weighing tenders. One such was No. 61095, shown here at March. This engine was allocated to Lincoln depot at the time, a shed that had a number of these very useful locomotives in its allocation for many years. Note the LMR 4F No. 43888 in the background, a class that became familiar at March, especially from the early sixties onwards after Peterborough Spital Bridge closed.

21.7.63

By late 1963, most of the passenger trains over Shap were diesel-hauled, many with the class 40s, including such trains as the 'Royal Scot'. Steam was usually to be found on heavy goods, parcels and fast goods traffic, with occasional appearances on special or weekend-only trains. 8F No. 48136 makes easy going on the northbound climb, banked by a Fairburn 2–6–4 tank.

'Schools' class No. 30913 *Christ's Hospital* roars through Clapham junction. This class of 4–4–0s was the last of this wheel arrangement built for use in the British Isles. They were introduced in 1930 to a Maunsell design for the Southern Railway. A few examples were fitted with large diameter chimneys, altering their appearance considerably.

The Scottish Region Beattock depot was only a small depot, several of its allocation being employed mainly on banking duties on Beattock bank. One of the engines was Fairburn 2–6–4T No. 42693.

18.9.64

Wellingborough Class 5 No. 44815 had worked in on a special and was still carrying its reporting number. The locomotive was serviced at March before a return working to the London Midland Region. Class 5 4–6–0s were a regular sight at March, especially in the sixties.

Standard class 4MT No. 75020 leaves Portmadoc. The high running-plate, allowing easy servicing and maintenance, was a design feature of the Standard class locomotives.

25.6.62

York A1 No. 60138 *Boswell* leaves Huntingdon. The A1s were introduced by Peppercorn, being a development of A1/1 No. 60113 *Great Northern* rebuilt by Thompson in 1945. After spending a number of years at York, *Boswell* was withdrawn in 1965.

24.2.63

Just a few years prior to this picture being taken, the ashpits at Oxford would have been a very busy scene. 'Hall' class No. 5923 *Colston Hall* was the only locomotive present, although several others were to be seen in the vicinity of the shed.

March yard as a shadow of its former self – in the past this part of the depot would have been packed with engines. WD No. 90722 was a Normanton engine. Just visible in the background are a class 5 and two B1 4–6–0s. From the mid-sixties onwards as many locomotives of LMS design were often present as those of Eastern and Standard designs together, especially after the closure of Peterborough Spital Bridge depot in January 1960.

28.7.63

The 4300 class Moguls were widely distributed throughout the Western Region, including Mid-Wales. At Barmouth, No. 6339 awaits its next duty. This class was first introduced in 1911, a Churchward design for the Great Western Railway. Moguls performed much valuable work on the Mid-Wales service.

7.61

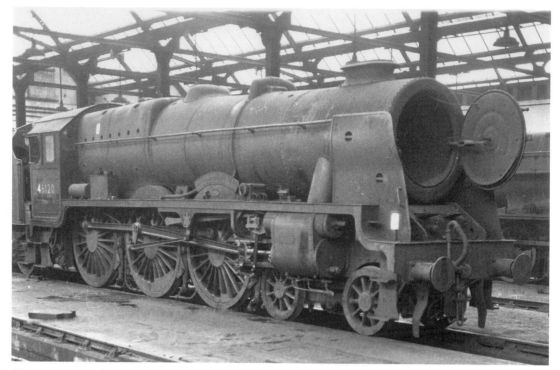

Bletchley depot had been called upon for repairs to 'Royal Scot' class No. 46120 *Royal Inniskilling Fusilier*. At this time the 'Scots' were mostly in a badly run-down condition. Whatever had happened to No. 46120 may have led to its demise, as the locomotive was withdrawn at Crewe in July 1963. It was cut up just three months later.

30.6.63

No. 92171 nears Peterborough. Long heavy-goods trains were still a familiar sight in the early sixties. The 9F 2–10–0s made light work of such trains on the east coast main line.

10.62

Several examples of the Standard 9F 2–10–0 present at Kettering shed on a Sunday. Included among them was No. 92102, which was a Wellingborough engine at this time. The Standard class 9F was a highly successful design found in many parts of the country. When first introduced they were subject to braking problems. These were soon rectified after tests on the east coast main line.

8.64

Class 5 No. 44937 at Shap. By this time steam locomotives on passenger trains were becoming rare, most having been replaced by class 40 diesels. No. 44937, a Carlisle Kingmoor locomotive, was attacking the climb unaided and in fine style with its ten-coach train.

9.63

No. 7911 *Lady Margaret Hall* is a member of the 6959 class 'Modified Hall' introduced in 1944, with larger superheater one-piece frames and plate-framed bogie, of which seventy-one examples were built. This Oxford engine is pictured outside its home depot.

9.63

A3 No. 60056 *Centenary* was a Grantham engine for many years, until withdrawal from that depot in October 1963. Here it is heading a Sunday local passenger train at Huntingdon, a return working from King's Cross. The engine ended its days at Doncaster works.

4.6.63

The Stanier 5MT 2–6–0 Moguls were introduced by the LMS in 1933 with just forty examples built. Occasionally they could be seen during the sixties at March. No. 42971 was at this time an Alsager engine, here at 31B depot.

21.6.64

One of New England's 9Fs, No. 92181, heads north on the 'Down slow' at Huntingdon, heading a long train of coal empties from Ferme Park. When new, several of the first locomotives built to this design were based at New England. Standard 9F 2–10–0s were eventually to be found in many parts of the country, with 251 examples in service.

One of Workington's 'Jinties', No. 47373, takes a breather. Note the once familiar shunter's pole lying on the front buffer beam. These 3F 0–6–0 tanks were the Standard LMS shunting locomotives. They were introduced in 1924, with eventually over four hundred in service.

Track-lifting duties kept this unfitted example of the J15 class active long after others had been withdrawn. No. 65420 is seen here at Godmanchester on the Huntingdon to St Ives line, ready to work back towards Huntingdon East. After each day's work the J15 ran light the twenty or so miles to New England depot.

31.8.61

In immaculate condition, A4 No. 60014 *Silver Link* was just four months away from withdrawal from service when photographed heading a northbound express on the 'Down slow' at Huntingdon. This King's Cross A4 was among the first members of the class to be withdrawn and was cut up at Doncaster works in 1963.

30.8.62

One of Tebay depot's bankers, No. 42110, assists a heavy northbound goods over the notorious wild open spaces of Shap incline. Most heavy freights would pick up a banker at Tebay; only lightly loaded goods trains would 'go it alone'. Several of the 2–6–4Ts were employed in this work.

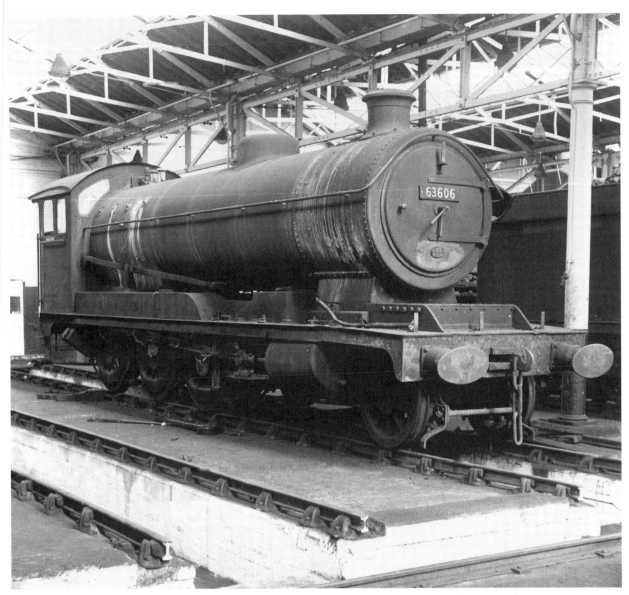

Here, the New England repair shop is carrying out work on Frodingham depot's 04/8 No. 63606. The coupling rods have already been removed. This engine shows signs of hard work on the smokebox door, and the front running-plate is bent – not an uncommon sight. No. 63606 was withdrawn the following year.

30.8.64

In the last years of steam working, a great many special trains were organized, often using locomotives from other regions. One of these was the 'Home Counties Railway Societies Special' to York, seen here at Peterborough. The Britannia No. 70020 *Mercury* was allocated to 1A Willesden at the time. For a number of years it was one of the batch allocated to Cardiff.

4.10.64

The 9F is capable of a fair turn of speed. Normally seen on goods workings, they occasionally worked parcels traffic on the east coast main line. Here, No. 92146 is seen heading south at speed.

4.10.62

2 Stored and Withdrawn Prior to 1965

The K3 class was easily recognized by its large-diameter boiler. It had a well-deserved reputation for rough riding when run-down and due for major overhaul. K3s were allocated to a considerable number of Eastern and Scottish region depots in British Railways days. March had several, including Nos 61942 and 61915, seen here stored.

26.5.63

Withdrawn 2251 class 0–6–0 No. 2236 at Machynlleth (89C) depot. This shed had an allocation of these very useful engines for a great many years, with four usually being sub-shedded at Aberystwyth. This class numbered 120 locomotives in total, with examples to be found at many Western Region depots.

March depot received a number of 'Britannias' when they were replaced elsewhere. No. 70030 *William Wordsworth* had been placed in store in the shed yard. Note the piece of tarpaulin tied over the chimney, and the fully-coaled tender. This 'Britannia' was eventually restored to traffic and worked on the London Midland Region until withdrawn from service.

23.6.63

The depot at March had for a number of years been known for stored or withdrawn locomotives. At this time, several were to be found in various parts of the yard, including this batch headed by J20 No. 64699. Next in line is J17 No. 65582, followed by K3s Nos 61915 and 61942. In recent years, numerous withdrawn diesel locomotives have spent long periods at March.

25.5.63

Carlisle Upperby yard contained a great many withdrawn locomotives. Included among them were 'Coronation' class Pacifics, 'Royal Scots', rebuilt 'Patriots' and many 4F 0–6–0s, a line of which is in the background. No. 46110 *Grenadier Guardsman* had been withdrawn in February 1964 and was scrapped in December of that year.

9.64

Among the Pacifics stored in New England yard was A3 No. 60044 *Melton*. This locomotive was withdrawn from service the following month, remaining stored until September when it was dispatched to Doncaster works. It was cut up two months later.

23.6.63

The Midland 3F 0–6–0 was a sizeable class with several variations. No. 43766 is an example of the design introduced in 1885 by Johnson, rebuilt from 1916 onwards with Belpaire boilers. This engine was a well-known Bedford depot locomotive. At this stage the possibility of the engine going back into service must still have existed, as the tender is fully coaled and the chimney protected.

This J72 was a long way from where the class would normally have been found. No. 68750 was among the withdrawn locomotives at Dumfries depot. This Scottish Region depot had an allocation of thirty or more engines. In the fifties these included a J69 Great Eastern 0–6–0T, one of several to be found in Scotland at that time.

9.63

With their duties taken over by diesels, several 'Coronation' class Pacifics were to be found lying out of use at Carlisle Upperby depot in late 1964. No. 46225 *Duchess of Gloucester* was one of them. Official withdrawal took place in the following month. The locomotive was later dispatched to Troon for scrapping, where it was cut up the following December.

18.9.64

By 1963 withdrawn locomotives were commonplace at a great many depots. Some were used for spares, as appears to have happened with 'Hall' class No. 5926 *Grotrian Hall* at Banbury. The safety-valve cover, smokebox handles, front buffers and all plates are missing. Doubtless other parts, not visible, would have been used also.

9.63

A2/3 No. 60500 *Edward Thompson* among the stored engines at New England. The following month this engine was withdrawn, ending its days at Doncaster works. For many years it was allocated to New England, often working semi-fasts to London along with other members of the class at this Eastern Region depot.

23.6.63

This J21 class engine, No. 65033, was the last of its class to be withdrawn. It was intended for preservation and was to be seen in Darlington works yard for several years. No. 65033, built in 1889, is pictured there during a works visit in 1964, having been withdrawn in April 1962. It had previously escaped scrapping in 1939 – owing to the war it was reinstated and continued in service for another twenty-three years.

2.5.64

A1 No. 60123 *H.A. Ivatt* had come to grief working a northbound fast goods at Offord on 7 September 1962. Here the locomotive is in sidings near the station two days later, ready to make its final journey north to Doncaster works where it was condemned and cut up in October.

9.9.62

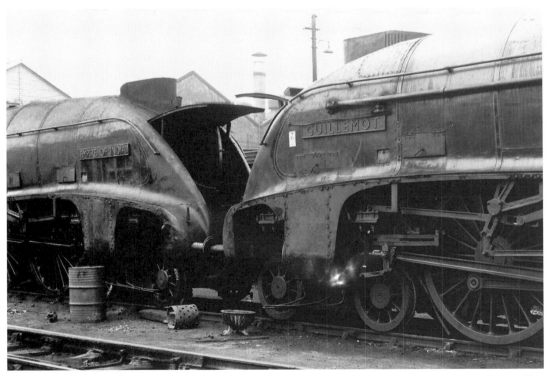

Neither of these two A4 Pacifics, pictured in Darlington works yard, were to be returned to traffic. No. 60011 *Empire of India* was in the process of undergoing examination, only to be condemned. No. 60020 *Guillemot* had already been withdrawn. *Empire of India* was for years a Haymarket depot engine and a frequent visitor to London. *Guillemot*, however, was a Gateshead locomotive and was only occasionally seen in the capital.

2.5.64

Only close inspection identified 'Castle' class No. 7030 *Cranbrook Castle* lying withdrawn at Oxford depot. This locomotive was built in 1950, and just thirteen years later was awaiting its last journey, as were several other locomotives at Oxford depot at this time.

9.63

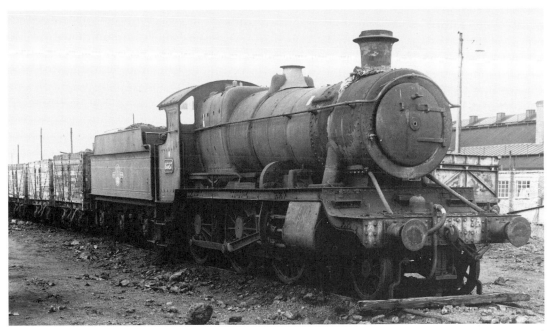

Slowly rusting away in Banbury yard was 4300 class Mogul No. 6367, giving the appearance of having been in store for some time. At one stage the chimney was probably covered, although whatever was used seems to be lying loose nearby. The front number-plate and smokebox door handles are missing. Rather surprisingly the brass cab-side number-plates were intact.

9.63

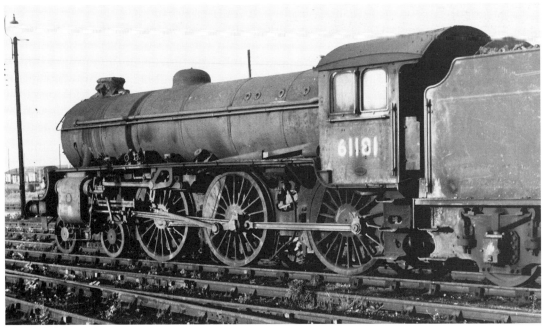

B1 No. 61181 was among the considerable number of stored locomotives at March. The B1 is complete, even with coal in the tender, and no doubt could have been returned to traffic quickly. March was one of the few depots still covering the chimney of stored locomotives with waterproof material at this time, once a common sight at Eastern and other regional depots.

9.63

Locomotives en route for scrapping could sometimes take a considerable time to reach their final destination. One such was Southern Region W class 2–6–4T No. 31924 on its way to Cohens, Kettering. Here it is at Wellingborough depot on 8 November 1964, where it had been for some time. By 22 November it had reached Kettering shed yard where it stood in company with a Western 72XX class 2–8–2 tank.

8.11.64

Stored next to 'Britannia' No. 70030 was 01 class No. 63780, having received the same protective treatment. Both are fully coaled and ready to be placed back in service at short notice. Since the early sixties, March has had a reputation for stored locomotives. In recent times, lines of long-since withdrawn diesels have been stored there.

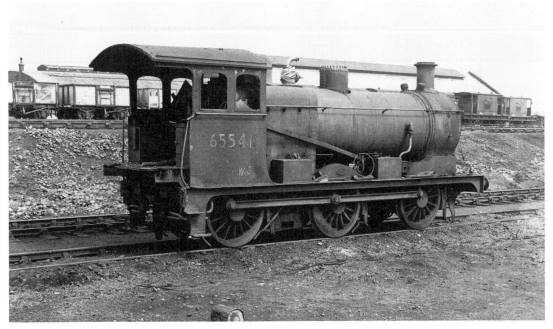

J17 No. 65541 had been in use as a stationary boiler at March depot. Now, having been replaced with another locomotive, it has been towed into the yard to await disposal. Many locomotives were employed on such duties after withdrawal from service at depots, carriage sheds, works, etc. Note the modifications made on top of the boiler for this purpose.

For a number of years a Carlisle-based engine, No. 46226 *Duchess of Norfolk* awaits its fate with No. 46250 *City of Lichfield* at Upperby depot. Several 'Coronation' Pacifics were either stored or withdrawn in the yards of the depot at this time. Both of these were dispatched to West of Scotland Shipbreaking Co., Troon.

18.9.64

Very few 2P 4–4–0s remained in service in late 1963. No. 40670 was stored at Dumfries. These locomotives were used on secondary services, cross-country lines and even as pilots on heavy expresses for a great many years. Unfortunately, none survive.

Several LMR 4F 0–6–0s were stored at March towards the end of steam working. This one, No. 44273, had lost its number-plate and, judging by the pile of coal in the foreground, the tender had recently been emptied, indicating that the locomotive had been withdrawn.

By 1963 even the very versatile B1 4–6–0s were finding themselves in storage. One member of the class in this situation at March was No. 61200. Presumably March depot thought it a possibility that this B1 would work again as it was fully coaled and protected.

26.5.63

A collection of scrap locomotives awaiting transfer to Cohens at Kettering shed. Among them was 7200 class 2–8–2T No. 7218, a heavy freight tank design introduced in 1934. These engines were rebuilds of Churchward 4200 design 2–8–0 tanks. Next in line is No. 31924, a W class 2–6–4T from the Southern Region.

22.11.64

With the closure of King's Cross depot to steam in 1963, several locomotives were moved to New England and placed in store in the shed yard. These comprised A3s and V2s, which were joined by two A2s allocated to New England. Here, V2 No. 60854 heads a line.

23.6.63

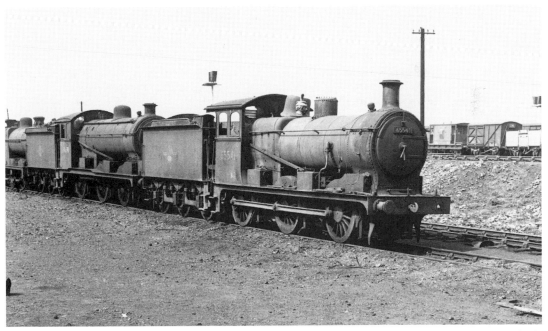

Withdrawn 0–6–0s wait for their final journey from March. Heading the line is J17 No. 65541 which had been in service as a stationary boiler. Note the dome on top of the boiler in front of the cab. The locomotive was also missing one of its front buffers. March depot was a sizeable shed with large yards. In its heyday the depot would contain a great many locomotives, especially at weekends. However, by 1963 the number had been greatly reduced.

23.6.63

Although exposed to the elements for some time, No. 6367 was still in lined green livery. The 4300 class Moguls were used on a variety of duties, including goods traffic, parcels, passenger duties, cross-country services, and even football and rugby specials.

9.63

Another of the 'Britannias' to be stored at March in 1963 was No. 70003 *John Bunyan*. Close inspection of the valve gear indicated that it had been liberally greased, although the rest of the locomotive was in a shabby condition. The March 'Britannias' were all returned to traffic and worked, mainly in the north-west.

3 The Final Four Years

The carriage sidings at Clapham Junction were a busy place and in steam days always attracted attention. Several Standard 4MTs were on empty stock workings to and from Waterloo. No. 80012 was one of them. Here it is leaving with a train of gleaming stock bound for Waterloo.

3.3.66

The Ivatt 2MT 2–6–2Ts were to be found in many parts of the country during their last years. No. 41298 was at Weymouth. This locomotive was one that had been fitted with a taller chimney, some of the tender version 2–6–0 Moguls also having this type of chimney.

26.3.66

The sturdy USA 0–6–0 tanks were a US Army Transportation design introduced in 1942. In 1946 the Southern Railway purchased fourteen, many of which were used on Southampton docks after cab and bunker modifications. Several spent their last days in service working for the Engineer's Department. One of those working at Redbridge sleeper depot (formerly No. 30061) was DS 233, seen here at Eastleigh motive power depot.

12.3.67

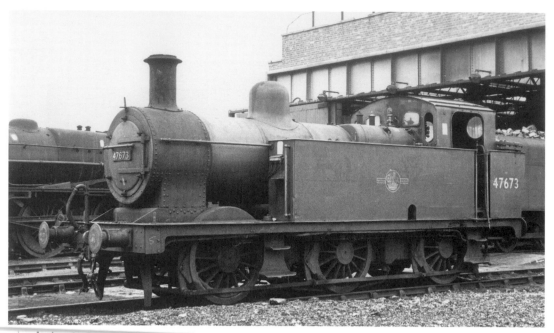

Llandudno junction was not a large shed, even in the fifties. However, summer weekends would usually find several additional locomotives 'on shed', with visitors from different areas working in on excursions and holiday specials throughout the summer season. One 'Jinty' was usually to be found at the depot, including No. 47673.

12.6.66

A4 No. 60024 *Kingfisher* was at the head of the 'A4 Preservation Society Special' to Weymouth on 20 March 1966. Here it is at the photo stop at Hamworthy junction. The return journey was via Dorchester West to Yeovil Pen Mill, where the A4 ran round its train before proceeding to Yeovil junction (with another run round). From here it went via Templecombe to Salisbury, where water was taken, before a memorable fast run back to London.

20.3.66

'Merchant Navy' No. 35007 *Aberdeen Commonwealth* is here under repair at Weymouth. Working on these locomotives outside in all weathers must have presented difficulties, being especially unpleasant during the winter months. Although still in service in 1967, this engine was not one of the lucky survivors. It was withdrawn in July and then dispatched to Buttigiegs, Newport where it ended its days.

26.3.66

Shortly before withdrawal, un-rebuilt 'Battle of Britain' class No. 34086 *219 Squadron* was dumped at the rear of Weymouth shed. Here it is pictured, minus one set of driving wheels and valve gear. Although name-plates, smokebox and number-plates were still in position, many of the locomotives in service at this time were missing various items.

26.3.66

5700 class Panniers withdrawn from service stand at Ebbw junction depot. The one here is No. 3767. Note the typical Great Western coaling/water plant in the background. All too soon these Panniers would make their last journey. It was not unknown for a few examples from South Wales depots to run under their own steam to the scrapyard.

25.10.65

In company with a considerable number of diesels, Standard 9F No. 92094 awaits its next turn of duty at Wellingborough, which would almost certainly have been a northbound iron ore train. These powerful locomotives from Wellingborough depot worked much of this traffic in their last days. The 9Fs were among the most successful of the Standard designs, on occasion even working passenger trains.

Class 5 No. 45056 was one of the batch built in 1934 and remained in service for thirty-three years. Some of the last examples built only managed fourteen or fifteen years. No. 45056 was at Crewe South depot on 12 February 1967. Six months later its working days were over. Considerably more (842) class 5s were built than the other LMR workhorses, the Stanier 8F 2–8–0s.

12.2.67

Standard class locomotives performed much useful work on the Southern Region in the last days of steam. Standard 4MT No. 76006 awaits the 'right away' from Brockenhurst with a Weymouth train. Four examples of this class, which was built between 1952 and 1957, have been preserved.

16.9.66

This sturdy 0–4–0 tank design was introduced by Deeley for the Midland Railway in 1907, with ten examples being built. These locomotives weighed nearly 33 tons and were fitted with Walschaerts valve gear. Pictured in 1966 at Canklow, this locomotive, No. 41533, was among the oldest engines still intact. This side view shows clearly the neat proportions of the design. It was introduced for shunting duties where tight-radius curves were involved.

8.4.66

At Bolton depot on 17 March 1968, the engines remaining in service were some Standard class 5s, Stanier 'Black 5s' and 8F 2–8–0s. Even these had less than five months remaining in service before they made their final journey. No. 73040 was in reasonable external condition, indicating that it may recently have been used on a special train.

17.3.68

Class 5 No. 44800 had just been withdrawn when photographed at Lostock Hall depot. Although dumped in a siding, this 1944-built class 5 still had its front number-plate, the valve gear motion and coupling rods intact.

17.3.68

Fairburn 2–6–4T No. 42138 at Manningham. These very useful locomotives first appeared in 1945. They were a development of the Stanier design, having a shorter wheelbase and other alterations. They were also fitted with self-cleaning smokeboxes. Several members of the class remained in service almost to the end of steam operations on British Railways.

20.3.66

'Britannia' No. 70024 *Tornado* spent its early days at Newton Abbot depot. Here it was a Carlisle Kingmoor engine. Judging by its external condition, which was reasonable, it had recently been used on a special. The original name-plate had been removed, leaving just a stencilled substitute.

10.66

During the last years of steam working at Wellingborough depot the Standard 9F 2–10–0s and 8F 2–8–0s were very much in evidence. Long gone were the days when visitors could usually rely on several 2–6–6–2T Beyer-Garratts being present. No. 92094 was in a condition typical of these locomotives.

22.5.66

Standard class 4MT No. 76051 shunts at Harston sidings. Considerable iron ore traffic was still handled from this point. The locomotive carries no shed-plate, although Colk (Colwick) is stencilled on the smokebox door.

4.6.66

Class 5 No. 45004 was one of the class built prior to the onset of the Second World War, in this case in March 1935. The engine was standing outside Llandudno junction depot. The first locomotives of this extensive class designed by Stanier made their appearance in 1934.

12.6.66

Despite their rather modern appearance, the first examples of this 0F 0–4–0ST design were introduced by the LMS in 1932. These locomotives were a Kitson design prepared to Stanier's requirements. This engine was built in 1953, the first example of the second batch. Here at Canklow it was technically still in service. It was withdrawn the following December.

8.4.66

Here class 5 No. 44819 has just received attention in Crewe works. This engine was built in December 1944 and withdrawn from service in December 1967.

16.10.66

Two 'Merchant Navy' class Pacifics were under repair at Weymouth on 26 March 1966. These included No. 35007 *Aberdeen Commonwealth*, which was still carrying reporting numbers. This locomotive has not survived. It remained in service for just over a year before it ended its days in South Wales.

26.3.66

The Standard class 5s were popular locomotives and were found in all regions. A few were named, some after 'King Arthur' 4–6–0s which had been withdrawn, others having associated names. The class was introduced in 1951, Nos 73125–54 being fitted with Caprotti valve gear. The last survivor was No. 73069 which was based at Carnforth. No. 73040 is pictured at Bolton and was withdrawn in May 1968.

3.68

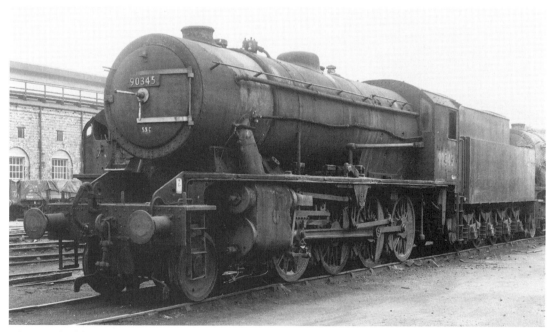

The invaluable WD 2–8–0s were still arriving at Crewe works for attention in October 1966. Here two await attention in the works yard. This class will long be remembered for the loud clanking sounds emitted when in motion. These engines were extensively used on many parts of British Railways, mostly on heavy goods trains.

10.66

The dull wet conditions do little to improve the appearance of 'West Country' class No. 34093 *Saunton* as it heads the 'Bournemouth Belle' through Brockenhurst on its way to London. The locomotive was in an appalling external condition, lacking its name-plate. It was withdrawn in July 1967 and ended its days after a year in store at Cashmores, Newport.

16.9.66

Class 5 No. 44883 of Carlisle Upperby depot (12A) was at Crewe South shed, fitted with a small snowplough. Time was running out for this class 5 as it had just five more months in service, giving a total of just twenty-two years.

12.2.67

The Lymington branch services were in the hands of Standard class 4MT 2–6–4 tanks in the mid-sixties. Here, No. 80085, minus its front number-plate, replenishes its water supply at Brockenhurst. During the fifties many such branches on the Southern Region were worked by M7 0–4–4Ts.

16.9.66

'Britannia' No. 70016 *Ariel* was at Leeds Holbeck depot in the company of two 'Peaks'. The 'Britannia' was a Carlisle Kingmoor locomotive and had worked down to Leeds over the Settle and Carlisle. Prior to moving to the LMR, *Ariel* had been allocated to Cardiff Canton depot. It was to remain in traffic for just over a year.

20.3.66

Among the last 8F 2–8–0s in service were these three standing outside Rose Grove depot. No. 48167, nearest the camera, and No. 48323, at the far end, are clearly work-stained. No. 48340 in the centre is in reasonable external condition and may have been cleaned for use on an enthusiasts' special, many of which were operated in the north-west at this time.

17.3.68

Class 5 No. 44800 at Banbury had recently received works attention. The engine survived in service for just over a further two years before being withdrawn from Lostock Hall shed.

25.9.66

Among the interesting collection of small tanks and locomotives which were in storage in the yard at Canklow depot were two of the 0–4–0Ts introduced by the Midland Railway in 1907. This class totalled just ten locomotives. Those at Canklow at this time were Nos 41528 and 41533.

8.4.66

'Britannia' class No. 70024 *Vulcan* moves off the turntable at Crewe South shed. The remaining 'Britannias' were to be seen working parcels and freight in their last years, with only occasional passenger trains, these being Saturday reliefs and specials. Note that the name-plate has already gone. In the background is Crewe South depot with a mixture of diesels, class 5s and 8Fs on shed.

16.10.66

Very typical of the condition in which many of the Bulleid Pacifics were to be seen during the mid-sixties, 'West Country' No. 34021 *Dartmoor* awaits its next duty at Weymouth depot. Note its deplorable condition, with name-plates removed, but surprisingly with the front number-plate remaining (missing on many in service at this time). This locomotive was not among the lucky survivors.

26.3.66

8F No. 48476 and Standard class 5 No. 73069 ready to work the Railway Correspondence and Travel Society's 'End of Steam' special to Blackburn, at Manchester Victoria. In the weeks prior to the final day, many specials were operated, some of which were bedevilled with problems and late running. This particular tour arrived back four hours late.

4.8.68

4 Some That Still Survive

Having just arrived in the capital with 'The Elizabethan', Haymarket depot A4 No. 60009 *Union of South Africa* leaves King's Cross for a well-earned rest and servicing before returning north the following day. This locomotive is one of the lucky survivors. On withdrawal in June 1966 from Aberdeen Ferryhill, it was purchased privately for preservation. No. 60009 is one of the most popular of all the steam locomotives on special workings.

9.61

In the yard at Shewsbury depot, 'Jubilee' class No. 45699 *Galatea* was just four months away from withdrawal. The engine was eventually to find itself at Barry where it remained for five years. In 1980 it was purchased and is now at the Severn Valley Railway. Still in a derelict condition, it is extremely unlikely that it will ever work again as it was purchased principally for spares.

21.7.64

Great Western 2–6–0 Mogul No. 5322 was the third locomotive to leave Barry, although it was to remain there for a further eight years after this 1965 photograph. This engine was built in 1917 and withdrawn in 1964. It is now preserved at Didcot Railway Centre, one of only two of the once numerous Great Western Moguls to survive.

25.10.65

S15 4–6–0 No. 30830 in 1965. Built at Eastleigh works in 1927, this engine had years of exposure to the salt-laden atmosphere of Barry ahead of it. It is now at the Bluebell Railway, very much in Barry condition, since no restoration work has been carried out to date.

25.10.65

This example of the 5205 class 2–8–0T, No. 5224, was remarkably intact at Barry on 25 October 1965. Built in 1924, it was withdrawn thirty-nine years later. The engine was purchased by the Great Central Railway, arriving at Loughborough in 1978. Since restoration it has been in regular use.

25.10.65

J27 class 0–6–0 No. 65894 was still very much in action at York depot on 2 May 1964, as it still is today on the North Yorkshire Moors Railway. It has been a visiting locomotive at several other preserved lines. The J27 class was first introduced by the North-Eastern Railway in 1906. No. 65894 was an example of the superheated piston valve locomotives introduced by Raven in 1921. It was the last built, in this case at Darlington in 1923, and is the only survivor of its type.

2.5.64

It seemed quite beyond the realms of all possibility that No. 71000, here pictured at Crewe, would be restored and one day haul passenger trains again. Fortunately, the locomotive was dispatched to Barry, from where it was rescued for preservation, albeit after seven years. It left South Wales for the Great Central Railway in 1974. Now, after a lengthy restoration (including new cylinders, etc.), *Duke of Gloucester* is one of the most popular of all preserved Pacifics.

16.10.66

Two privately-owned locomotives are pictured at Leeds Holbeck. In the
No. 69621. Although the British Railways emblem is still partially visible
The engine was built at Stratford in 1924. The only survivor of its class, i
on various occasions throughout the year.

For several months, No. 71000 *Duke of Gloucester* was to be seen partially dismantled in Crewe works
yard. The cylinders and valve gear were removed for preservation and display. Pictured here are the
remains prior to their removal to Woodham Brothers at Barry, where they remained for a number of
years before their rescue. No. 71000 was built in May 1954, the sole example of the class 8P Standard
Pacific design. The engine was withdrawn from service in December 1962.

16.10.66

2800 class 2-8-0 No. 3862, one of the batch fitted with side-wind considerable number of years exposed to the elements at Barry before of sixteen 2800 class locomotives that have survived. No restoration engine.

Visitors to Barry in 1965 would never have thought it possible that this 'Castle' class locomotive, No. 5080 *Defiant*, would ever haul express passenger trains again. Fortunately it does, and *Defiant* is now to be seen in excellent condition. The engine was built at Swindon in 1939 and originally named *Ogmore Castle*. It is now at the Birmingham Railway Museum.

25.10.65

Just fourteen years after this photograph, 5101 class 2-6-2T Prairie No. 5164 was back in steam. Designed by Collett, this locomotive was completed in November 1930. It was withdrawn from service in April 1963 and its departure from Barry for preservation followed ten years later. No. 5164 is part of the locomotive stud of the Severn Valley Railway.

25.10.65

'Merchant Navy' class No. 35025 *Brocklebank Line* was withdrawn from service at Exmouth junction depot. It had been at Barry for just seven months when this photograph was taken. The engine is now at the Great Central Railway, Loughborough, awaiting attention.

25.10.65

Another of the 'Halls' at Barry was No. 5952 *Cogan Hall*, built at the famous Swindon works in 1935. Sixteen years of lying at Barry exposed to the elements lay ahead for this engine. The locomotive is now at the Llangollen Railway awaiting restoration.

25.10.65

5 Point of No Return

Push-pull-fitted 2MT No. 41228 was one of several 2MT tanks in the process of being scrapped at Cohens on 8 November 1964. Increasing numbers of diesel sets and the closure of many services resulted in a considerable number of these very useful steam locomotives becoming redundant.

8.11.64

This sad scene could easily be entitled 'Guess this class'. It shows one of the few Southern Region locomotives that found their way to Cohens, Kettering. The remains are those of V class 'Schools' 4–4–0 No. 30935 *Sevenoaks*, a Maunsell design introduced in 1930. This was the last new design of this wheel arrangement to appear in the British Isles.

5.7.64

Little remains of No. 44113's tender, here pictured on 25 May 1966. These very useful locomotives were to be found throughout the London Midland and in parts of the Scottish regions, and in later years on the Eastern Region. This particular locomotive completed forty-one years of service.

25.5.66

Stripped of all cab fittings, a sad row of locomotives await their fate at Cohens. In the foreground is No. 75041, next in line class 5 No. 44889, and the last locomotive, another class 5, No. 44678, which managed just seventeen years of service.

9.5.68

Some Eastern Region locomotives, found their way to Cohens, mostly B1 class 4–6–0s and 2–8–0 heavy freight designs. Here B1 No. 61145 is in the process of being cut up. The workmen in this case began at the cab end first.

17.4.66

Withdrawn locomotives that arrived at Cashmores Newport yard were quickly cut up. On 25 October 1965 those awaiting their fate consisted of two Standard tanks, a 9F and a 'Hall' class 4–6–0. Nos 82037 and 92237 are pictured in a siding. The Standard 3MT tank class is another of those classes where no example has survived into preservation.

25.10.65

The sad remains of 'Jinty' No. 47535 lie at Cohens. Within a short time nothing would remain of this locomotive. The dome and sections of the boiler barrel and smokebox are to be seen scattered around. This picture gives a good view of the firebox fitted to these locomotives.

W class No. 31914 at Cohens. All three of the W class 2–6–4Ts that arrived here, Nos 31912, 31914 and 31924, were in reasonable condition. The locomotives at either end are class 4F 0–6–0s, a great many of which ended their days here.

15.11.64

Standard class 9F No. 92237 is pictured at Cashmores, Newport. Note that it still has its valve and running gear, mostly intact. This locomotive is one of those with a double chimney. Nine examples of this class still survive. They included No. 92220 *Evening Star*, the last locomotive built for British Railways, being constructed at Swindon works in 1960.

25.10.65

Fairburn 2–6–4T No. 42133 and class 5 No. 45147 await their fate at Cohens, Kettering. In the background are further examples. Other 2–6–4 tanks in the sidings included Nos 42086 and 42233. Over the years this scrapyard received locomotives from the Western, Southern, London Midland and Eastern regions.

1.10.67

'Modified Hall' class No. 6973 *Bricklehampton Hall* stands ready to be moved into position at Cashmores, Newport for repairs. The 'Modified Halls' were introduced by Hawksworth in 1944, with seventy-one being constructed. The class was a development of the earlier 'Hall' class which made its first appearance in 1924.

25.10.65

Still in remarkably good external condition, W class 2–6–4T No. 31912 awaits its fate. Several of these attractive locomotives were based in the London area and used on inter-regional freights, stock workings, etc. Hither Green depot had a number of these engines. The class was introduced in 1931 and consisted of fifteen locomotives numbered 31911 to 31925. Unfortunately, none has survived into preservation.

8.11.64

Standard class 4 2–6–0 Mogul No. 76036 had arrived at Cohens from Chester, its last allocation. Many of the Standard classes were in service for as little as twelve years. The high running-plate on this design enabled easier maintenance. In the five-year period from 1952 to 1957, 115 locomotives of this design were built.

While many 'Jinties' ended their days at Cohens, only one example of the 'Johnson Halfcab' 0–6–0T appears to have arrived there. Here is No. 41712 on a rainy December day in 1964. This locomotive had been rebuilt with a Belpaire boiler, but still retained its rather spartan cab.

12.64

Locomotives of various types tended to come to Cohens in batches. On 1 October 1967 several 2–6–4Ts were on the site. This one is Fairburn design No. 42233. Work was under way to remove the boiler tubes.

1.10.67

Cohens, Kettering was in the process of scrapping a batch of 4F 0–6–0s. The chimney of another member of the class is lying in the foreground. Over the years a large number of 4Fs ended their days here, including this one, No. 44113, which was built in 1925.

25.5.66

4F No. 44278 had been waiting to be scrapped at Cohens for several weeks. On 22 May 1966 it had reached this stage and within days would be reduced to scrap metal. This locomotive was one example of the class running with a tender cab.

22.5.66

Two Fairburn 2–6–4 tanks, Nos 42133 and 42086, stand in the sidings at Cohens surrounded by various London Midland Region locomotives. This design was introduced in 1945 and was a development of the earlier Stanier type, with a shorter wheel base and other modifications.

1.10.67

This picture of W class No. 31912 has been included as it shows that although an engine might be in a scrapyard progress could be slow. Only part of the cab bunker and the front of the tank have gone. Other locomotives had been reduced to a pile of metal. In the background is Cohens own locomotive, used to move engines around.

8.10.67

Many 4F 0–6–0s of the London Midland Region made their last journey to Cohens. Here is No. 44441 with one of the later Standard Midland tenders. Note the diagonal yellow line on the cab-side, warning of electrified lines. This engine was one of several 4Fs present.

15.11.64

Class 5s arrived at Kettering in a variety of conditions. Apart from broken cab windows, No. 45240 appeared more or less intact, although many cab fittings had been removed. Note the connecting rod tied onto the running-plate.

'Jinties' arrived at Kettering over a long period. No. 47355, pictured at Cohens in January 1965, was typical of this numerous LMS shunting tank design, of which 417 were in service in 1952. Introduced in 1924, they were a post-Grouping development of an earlier Midland design.

1.65

In 1967 several 'Jinties' arrived for scrapping at Cohens, Kettering. Among these No. 47482, pictured here, had the distinction of carrying its number on the side of the tank. This was the only example, the number having been applied at Darlington works in North-Eastern tradition.

5.2.67

One of the locomotive classes that surely deserved at least one example in preservation was the 6800 'Grange' class which was introduced in 1936. Unfortunately, not one has survived. Several members of this class ended up at Cohens. This one, having just lost its boiler tubes, is No. 6839 *Hewell Grange*.
15.11.64

This sad scene at Cohens is typical of the end of many once-proud steam locomotives. The method by which the job was tackled seemed to depend very much on the personnel concerned. These remains are of 2MT No. 41228. Note the chimney lying in the foreground, with tubes and numerous bits and pieces. Note also that the firebox is still more or less intact at this stage.

Ivatt 2–6–0 Mogul No. 46495 ended its days at Cohens scrapyard, Kettering. For most of its life this engine was allocated to 15B Kettering depot. Up to the closure of the line in 1959 it was one of the regular engines on the Cambridge service. Here it awaits its fate.

5.2.67